CLASSIC ROCK CLIMBS
NUMBER 26

McConnells Mill State Park

PENNSYLVANIA

by
Bob Value

CHOCKSTONE

FALCON®

HELENA, MONTANA

A FALCON GUIDE®

Falcon® Publishing is continually expanding its list of recreation guidebooks. All books include detailed descriptions, accurate maps, and all the information necessary for enjoyable trips. You can order extra copies of this book and get information and prices for other Falcon® guidebooks by writing Falcon, P.O. Box 1718, Helena, MT 59624 or calling toll free 1-800-582-2665. Also, please ask for a free copy of our current catalog. Visit our website at www.falcongutdoors.com.

©1999 Bob Value
Printed in the United States of America

1 2 3 4 5 6 7 8 9 0 MG 04 03 02 01 00 99

ISBN 1-57540-025-1 *Classic Rock Climbs* series
    1-56044-756-7 *Classic Rock Climbs #26: McConnells Mill State Park, Pennsylvania*

Falcon, FalconGuide, and Chockstone are registered trademarks of Falcon® Publishing, Inc.

Cover: Bobby Simmons on *Mini Ovest*. Photo by Carl Samples.

Library of Congress Cataloging-in-Publication Data

Value, Bob
    McConnells Mill State Park / by Bob Value.
                    p.   cm. -- (Classic rock climbs ; no. 26)   (A Falcon guide)
        ISBN 1-56044-756-7 (pbk. : alk. paper)
            1. Rock climbing–Pennsylvania–McConnells Mill State Park–
    Guidebooks. 2. McConnells Mill State Park (Pa.)--Guidebooks.
    I. Title. II. Series. III. Series: A Falcon guide.
    GV199.42.P42M336   1999
    798.52'23'0974893--dc21
                                                                                98-3741
                                                                                CIP

CAUTION

Outdoor recreational activities are by their very nature potentially hazardous. All participants in such activities must assume the responsibility for their own actions and safety. The information contained in this guidebook cannot replace sound judgment and good decision-making skills, which help reduce risk exposure, nor does the scope of this book allow for disclosure of all the potential hazards and risks involved in such activities.

Learn as much as possible about the outdoor recreational activities in which you participate, prepare for the unexpected, and be cautious. The reward will be a safer and more enjoyable experience.

 Text pages printed on recycled paper.

In memory of Keith "Fingers" Biearman;
a good friend, climbing partner and a long-time
fixture in the local climbing community.

ACKNOWLEDGMENTS

When assembling a guidebook of this nature, one's job description becomes that of editor rather than author. Many individuals provided input that hopefully adds objectivity and certainly lends character to the book. The following is a partial list of contributors who made the guide possible:

A special thanks goes out to Rick Thompson and Carl Samples. Rick (aka Rico), in addition to providing the maps for this guide (all hand-drawn in his unique style), was a prime motivator in doing the book. Rico provided significant help with route history as well as technical input on design and layout. He also whipped me back into shape after a lengthy sabbatical. Carl, whose wonderful photos can be found in calendars, magazines and other guidebooks, made numerous pilgrimages to the Mill to take many of the photos that grace these pages. The photos were taken in difficult, low-light conditions and are a statement of his artistic and technical abilities behind a camera. To Bill Crick, my oldest friend and climbing partner—thank you for taking the time to compare notes on route histories. Finally, a special thank you to my long-suffering wife, Dawn, whose eyes are permanently rolled into the backs of her sockets from years of bearing with my various escapades.

The following individuals were involved either in providing first ascent information, route information, grading consensus, and/or proofreading text, and all the other behind-the-scene elements of putting together this guide-book: Kurt and Sharon Byrnes, Chris Eckstein, Ivan Jirak, Ron Kampas, Shawn McGuirk, Dean Morgan, Mark Van Cura and Dick Watson.

My sincere thanks to the many climbers not listed who have given up precious time while at the crag to provide input on grades and other information.

TABLE OF CONTENTS

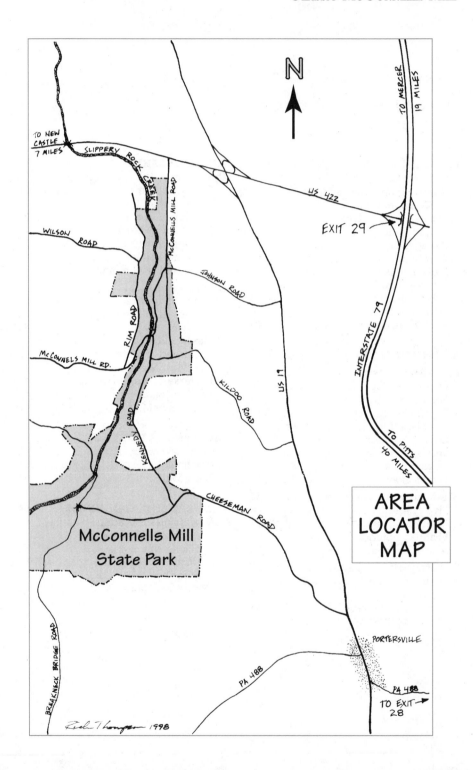

AREA
LOCATOR
MAP

INTRODUCTION

McConnells Mill

McConnells Mill State Park is a popular climbing area located in Lawrence County, Pennsylvania, approximately 40 miles north of Pittsburgh. It is easily accessed from the north or south via Interstate 79, or from the east or west via State Route 422. The focal points of the park are the restored gristmill, the covered bridge, and the dramatic glaciated gorge that surrounds these structures for several miles up and downstream.

Daniel Kennedy built the existing mill in 1868 to replace his original mill that was destroyed by fire. The covered bridge was built in 1874 and is a Howe Truss bridge. It is one of two covered bridges still in existence in Lawrence County. In 1875, Thomas McConnell bought the mill from Kennedy and replaced the original water wheel and grinding stones with water turbines and rolling mills. The modernized mill was one of the earliest rolling mills in the country and processed a variety of locally grown grains until it closed in 1928. Ownership of the mill, along with its surrounding property, was eventually conveyed from Thomas Hartman to the Western Pennsylvania Conservancy and later to the Commonwealth. McConnells Mill became a state park in 1957 and was given National Natural Landmark status in 1974.

The steep Slippery Rock Gorge was formed as the advancing Wisconsin Ice Sheet created ice dams on the Slippery Rock and neighboring Muddy Creek. As these dams receded, the resulting lakes drained through the Slippery Rock watershed, eroding the 400-foot deep gorge and exposing the sandstone outcrops along the rim. Time, gravity, and erosion have caused house-sized boulders to fall from the rim of the gorge and create the sandstone rock "cities" that today provide wonderful climbing.

In addition to rock climbing, many other recreational opportunities exist in the park. Ice climbing is available during good winters. Enthusiasts should visit the falls at Alpha Pass and the area of rock just upstream from there when conditions permit. Enterprising ice hounds can ferret out many other flows that sometimes form and become climbable. Whitewater rafting and kayaking are extremely popular activities on Slippery Rock Creek, as is fishing. The river is managed as a trout fishery but also has an excellent population of smallmouth

Kurt Byrnes on Smell the Glove, *Island Block.*
Photo by Carl Samples.

bass. For the purist, there is a delayed-harvest, fly fishing-only section about 2 miles downstream from the mill at the Armstrong Bridge. Approximately 7 miles of hiking trails exist and many areas of the park are open for hunting on a seasonal basis.

Camping is not available in the park, which is operated as a day use resource; however there are several private campgrounds located nearby. Coopers Lake is 1 mile east of the park off of State Route 422. Rosepoint Campground is 0.5 mile west on State Route 422, and recently a primitive campground—the "R Ranch"—opened on private property along Rim Road. It is located approximately 100 yards beyond the picnic table and parking area.

There is a recreational guide to the park that is available from the staff, which includes more detailed listings of the area's attractions, rules and regulations.

CLIMBING AND ENVIRONMENTAL CONSIDERATIONS Climbing in Pennsylvania state parks is a privilege. At this time, Ralph Stover and McConnells Mill (known to locals as the Mill) are the only Pennsylvania state parks where it is actually a sanctioned activity. **However, climbing at McConnells Mill is allowed only in designated areas. If you are caught climbing outside these areas you may receive a citation.**

NOTE: CLIMBING IS NOT CURRENTLY PERMITTED AT THE ROADSIDE CRAGS. The Roadside climbs are listed for historical reference only. Hopefully, by increasing climber interest in these areas and by taking a more proactive role in the park's policy formulation, we may someday see implemented a limited climbing and bouldering policy for this portion of the park.

Western Pennsylvania climbers have seen many significant climbing areas affected by access problems in recent years. Most of these areas are controlled by private landowners. Significantly, McConnells Mill is a publicly owned resource. If this guide whets your appetite and you'd like to see some of these closed routes re-opened, become an activist: Write the Pennsylvania Department of Conservation & Natural Resources, join the Access Fund, and become involved in future efforts to preserve and enlarge the scope of this climbing resource.

The cliffs at the Mill vary from 12 to 50 feet high, offering climbs of all angles. Vertical faces feature pockets, flakes, and the area's trademark — shallow sloping horizontals that often turn into a date with disappointment for the would-be ascentionist. On the other extreme, many of the testpieces climb very steep rock with bouldery cruxes between endurance sprints on jugs. Some of these steeper routes overhang almost as much as they extend upward. The rock is typically medium-textured sandstone, but very gritty sections as well as smoother-grained spots will be encountered.

Certain walls allow for excellent targeted workout circuits due to the similar nature of the routes. The east face of Island Block, for example, is ideal for working open-hand strength due to its steep angle and abundance of big moves off slopers and rounded pockets. Birthday Boulder serves up a theme of small crimpers, with a half-pad sized hold being a welcome rest.

Climbing conditions at the park are perhaps best described by the statement, "When it's good it's pretty decent, and when it's bad it's awful." The local weather patterns are unpredictable, and the rocks respond to precipitation in similarly unpredictable ways. Often I make the drive up expecting perfect conditions—it was dry yesterday when I climbed at the Mill, and it hasn't rained since then—and yet the rocks will somehow be oozing and wet. On other days the rock will be dry right after a heavy rain. The only way to tell is to make the pilgrimage. The rock does provide excellent friction when the conditions are right.

The best season for climbing is difficult to nail down. Winters are very cold but dry spells often provide great friction conditions on some of the harder boulder problems. Summers are typically shady but very humid. For two weeks in early June the park suffers from an invasion of gnats that seems to appear and then disappear overnight. Climbing conditions are generally good during this late spring period, but pack your insect repellent. Fall is probably the most stable time of the year, given the cool, dry, high-pressure systems that seem to prevail in the eastern United States during this time. Unfortunately, the cliffs also tend to be crowded because the local outing clubs bring in vanloads of college students for climbing classes.

The park, while maintaining its rugged character, is starting to show increasing signs of wear. Covered by a majestic canopy of tall hemlocks and carpeted with fragile mosses, popular areas in the park are suffering from tremendous soil erosion. A walk along the more popular trails, including the main climbing areas, will yield broken glass, cans, cigarette butts, and other assorted eyesores. Graffiti is also on the rise and the author encourages any climbers witnessing rock defacement to quietly go get one of the park employees. Even more distressing is the amount of climber garbage that is beginning to litter these areas. While it is easy for climbers to shrug off the litter problem as being caused primarily by non-climbers, as a group we are guilty of exacerbating the situation by leaving tape, old rugs, and other accouterments at the crag. The solution includes picking up any garbage that you encounter, whether it is yours or not.

The cliffs are heavily vegetated and all new routes will likely require some brushing. Before you launch into such a project, however, ask yourself this question: Will the quality of the route outweigh the visual and environmental impact that it will create? The reader will note that several routes in this guide have reverted to a vegetated state. Why? Because the quality of these routes was such that they did not get many, if any, repeat ascents. The routes were simply not worth the impact, and it has taken many years for the vegetation to return to some semblance of its pre-cleaned state.

People and ropes have heavily impacted the belay trees and the tops of many popular routes. Always use slings when anchoring to trees, and pad the slings with a rope bag or other items to minimize the wear and tear on the tree bark. DO NOT anchor your rope directly to trees. And don't rappel from trees and then attempt to pull the rope—the resulting abrasion causes significant damage. A carpet under your anchor rig at the top will not only save unnecessary abrasion on your equipment but will also provide some protection to the fragile soil at the top of the route. In addition to standard toproping paraphernalia, pack some extra long rigging slings.

Bolts are a difficult subject in the park. There is a sound argument for the use of top anchors as a conservation method that minimizes soil and vegetation impact on some of the cliffs. The top of Island Block, for example, is suffering significant soil and vegetation impact. Fixed anchors would go a long way toward solving this problem. On some remote, overhanging cliffs, fixed anchors have appeared. These isolated cases were the focus of much soul searching and debate by local activists. Their intent upon placing the bolts was not to create a "Euro Crag" but instead to prevent climbing accidents and further clifftop erosion—both of which seriously threaten access. At this time, locals agree that the use of bolts on any of the more popular, highly-visible cliffs is not acceptable.

Each year the popularity of the park increases and, given the rugged nature of the park and the diverse user groups, accidents have also been on the rise. While true technical climbing accidents are rare, the local press and the park administration tend to call all manner of accidents "climbing accidents." When tourists slip off the edge of the cliff it's called a "climbing accident," and even technical whitewater rescues are sometimes called "climbing accidents." At the same time, it is true that these cliffs are notoriously slippery when wet, and holds can unexpectedly snap. Practice safe climbing! And if you see other climbers (or non-climbers) in an unsafe situation, don't hesitate to get involved! The access you save may be your own!

Due to budget cuts, the already overworked park staff is now responsible for both McConnells Mill and nearby Moraine State Park. As with all things, Murphy's Law rules, meaning that when you need the staff the most, they may be hard to find. An emergency phone is located by the mill. This phone is for *true* 911 emergencies only! There is also a pay phone located at the north end of McConnells Mill Road by the park headquarters.

Charlie Rafferty upstream from The Mill.
Photo by Carl Samples.

The Mill should be considered a toprope and bouldering area, although there are some vertical cracks that competent climbers might consider leading. In general, the shallow pockets and horizontals that characterize the majority of the routes here are not conducive to safe leading and the tops of many of the cracks can be quite desperate grungefests if they have not been whisked recently. Besides, while the rock at the Mill is of generally sound quality, solid-looking flakes will sometimes explode in your hands after a soaking rain or during the spring thaw.

This brings up another subject. Many of the classic problems in the park have small pockets and edges that are very susceptible to breaking when they are wet. If you must climb during these times, please use extra care when pulling on them.

On the bouldering front, many problems listed are either high boulders or have potentially bad landings. Traditionally, new boulders have been done without toprope rehearsal. Routes such as *Son of Foops* or *Up Shit Crick* may seem trivial by today's technical standards, but the cruxy last moves come right when the air is starting to get a little thin. On other boulders, such as *Fall Safe Point*, the ledges and rocks at the bottom make failure an unpleasant option at best. A "sketch pad" might help defray the cost of failure; however, the most useful tools a climber can bring to the base of a high boulder problem are poise, control, and commitment. And remember that this guide is in no way a substitute for sound judgment, experience, and an understanding of a your own personal limits. CLIMB AT YOUR OWN RISK!

LEAVE NO TRACE OUTDOOR SKILLS AND ETHICS Leave No Trace is a national non-profit organization based in Boulder, Colorado that educates outdoor recreation user groups, federal agency personnel, and the public about minimum impact techniques. The following information is taken from their rock climbing booklet. Whether you're a backcountry trad-master or on the road to a 5.13 redpoint at the local crag, these principles and practices are for you. They are not rules, but rather guidelines based on climbers' abiding respect for and appreciation of wild and unique places and their inhabitants. To apply them effectively, they must be tempered with common sense and adapted to the specific environment or situation. Adventure, beauty, and the freedom to pursue our craft remain essential to climbers. Continued access to the crags and the freedom to choose the rules of our game depends on making Leave No Trace a part of our daily climbing routine.

American climbers have historically been a group with a high standard of environmental care. However, the ethic that carried us through the early days of climbing is not enough anymore due to the combined effects of an ever-growing number of climbers and ever-changing technologies. As an area's popularity increases, impacts to the land and to other visitors accelerate and become difficult to reverse. Litter, fire scars, and poorly planned trails are some of the unfortunate signs of carelessness that exist at some of our nation's climbing areas.

We are appealing to all climbers to accept personal responsibility for the care of our fragile resources. Toward this goal, we offer the following principles, developed through the collaborative efforts of climbers, land managers, and climbing organizations, including the Access Fund.

The Principles of Leave No Trace are:

• Plan Ahead and Prepare

• Camp and Travel on Durable Surfaces

• Pack It In, Pack It Out

• Properly Dispose of What You Can't Pack Out

• Leave What You Find

• Minimize Use and Impact from Fires

And for climbers they all add up to the seventh principle:

• Minimize Climbing Impacts

RATINGS The Yosemite Decimal System is used for all toprope problems. Boulder problems are rated using the popular "V" scale, which originated at Hueco Tanks, Texas. Efforts have been made to use consensus grades but several of the boulder problems and topropes have had few, if any, repeats. Many of the boulder problems may feel height-dependent, so don't be offended if you find that a particular problem feels easier or harder than the grade suggests. Below is a rough approximation of how the "V" scale compares to the Yosemite Decimal System; some examples of the park standard(s) for each grade are listed for reference. Boulder problems with obvious bad landings or long fall potential are given an "R" rating. Remember, all boulder falls are ground falls and just because a problem is not listed as "R" does not mean that a fall will not result in injury or death. Use your best judgment before committing yourself, and climb at your own risk!

V0- under 5.9	*Jail Bait*
V0 5.9	*Center Route* on Ross Boulder
V0+ 5.10a/b	*Sweet Dreams*
V1 5.10c/d	*Short Traverse* on Ross Boulder
V2 5.11a/b	*Snake Bit/Mud Bath*
V3 5.11c/d	*The Leper/Five Fingers Traverse*
V4 5.12a	*The Cutting Edge/S.T.A.N.C.*
V5 5.12b/c	*Birthday Boulder*
V6 5.12d	*The Burning Zone*

A three-star quality rating system is used throughout the guide. One star indicates that a route has enough redeeming historical or qualitative value to justify being on everyone's ticklist. Two stars indicate that a route is above average in quality, and three stars are reserved for the park classics. The star system is a comparison of route quality within the park, and thus a three-star route in the park would not necessarily be comparable to a three-star route in other areas.

CLIMBING HISTORY This guide began when I handed out a list to some of my friends who had not been climbing at the park recently; my intention was to entice them into sampling some of the new routes and boulders in the area. Later, after sharing route information with others during winter forays to the local indoor walls, it became clear that there was enough need and interest for information on the Mill to warrant expanding the scope of the guide to be a more comprehensive route listing. The route list eventually grew to include first ascent data if it was available.

It also became tiresome seeing the same climbers on the same climbs every time they were at the Mill and listening to them whine about how there wasn't anything new to climb in the park! The local climbing community will hopefully benefit from this attempt to take the pressure taken off a couple heavily congested areas. Climbers will now have the information they need to sample some of the excellent but lesser-known routes.

Often climbers come to the park, make a small bang by putting up a route, and then go quietly into the night. The reader will note the lack of history on many of the older (pre-1970s) routes; there are many routes listed with no name or first ascent data. While I did make an effort to collect this information, sometimes it was simply not available. If you have what you feel is pertinent route information, please don't kick back in your armchair and grumble about how Joe Gritstone climbed *Peace, Love and Granola* in 1968. Give us feedback for the next edition! Having been active in new route exploration of the Mill and other western Pennsylvania areas since 1971, I have a good understanding of the prevailing technical standards and the local players since that time. By combining this knowledge with the information provided by Ivan Jirak in various editions of the *Pittsburgh Area Climbers Guide*, published from 1955 to 1977, I have been able to assemble most of the pieces of the puzzle; however, there are still substantial gaps in the park's early climbing history.

Climbing has existed at the park since at least the 1940s. Dr. Ivan Jirak, an early pioneer in the Pittsburgh climbing scene, started climbing at the Mill in 1947 while attending Slippery Rock College. On weekends the Slippery Rock Chapter of the Pittsburgh Explorers Club would run climbing outings to Breakneck Rocks. The college would provide large quantities of food for the students who would then need to carry it "Sherpa" style, balanced on their heads, to the base of the cliff. Camping at that time was permitted and the group would bivouac under the large overhang on the North Wall. Later, members of the A.K.s and the Explorers Club were active in developing many of the moderate classics in the park.

In the early 1970s, climbing standards at the Mill were low, as were western Pennsylvania standards in general. Classics of the time included many of the moderate Breakneck cracks, such as *The Arete* (5.7+) and *Lean Across* (5.6) on Island Block, *Beginners' Face* (5.4), *Five Fingers Arete* (5.8), and *R.O.T.C. Route* (5.8). *Ross's Boulder* (V0+) was the bouldering testpiece at the time.

During this era, a small group of climbers living in the northern suburbs of Pittsburgh descended on the Mill like a pack of dingoes because of its close proximity and new-route potential. This group initially included Bill Crick, Doug Haver, Keith Biearman, myself and occasionally others. We began spending a tremendous amount of time at the park, largely due to the fact that most of us were too young to drive and it was the easiest place to which we could bum rides. Some other familiar faces at the cliffs during that time were Les Moore, Nick Ross, the brothers Tom & Jerry Ordons, Ed Francis, Al Moore, Don French, Ron Walsh, Bob Broughton, and others. It could be argued that for a time, area standards were set at the Mill and then eventually spread out to other western Pennsylvania crags such as White Rocks. Some early successes during this period included *Laid Back* (10b) and *Mr. Clean* (10c)—which firmly established the 5.10 standard in the park—and *Sweet Dreams* (V0+ R), which established the grade on the bouldering front. As the decade progressed, the number of active members of the pack also grew to include people such as Jack Nard, Eric Guerrin, Ron Kampas, Scott Garso, Glenn Thomas, and Rick Thompson. These climbers began marking their territory while other climbers drifted off in search of other pursuits.

The latter part of the 1970s saw classic testpieces such as *Mission Impossible* (10d), *Tarzan* (10b) and *Temptation* (11a) receive their maiden ascents. Of particular note during this period was Eric Guerrin's ascent of the *Mini Ovest* (11d), an intimidating, steep route that several climbers had been working on. After freeing the climb he called me and, in keeping with the Seneca Rocks' influence so prevalent among local climbers at that time, rated it 5.10+. Later, after doing the second ascent, I remarked to Eric that I thought it was "probably" 5.11. Two decades later it is rated consensus 5.11d.

It was during this period that Bill Crick and I started turning a good bit of our attention toward the park's bouldering potential. Inspired first by rumors, and then eventually by Pat Ament's biography of John Gill, we opened many classic problems. Ross Boulder received a scouring with more eliminates and variations than I could subject a reader to in this guide. Bill completed the *Five Fingers Traverse* (V3), and it was during this time that many of the best Roadside boulder problems such as *Son of Foops* (V2 R), *Mud Bath* (V2) and *Up Shit Crick* (V0+ R) were done. The decade culminated with ascents of *Smell The Glove* (V3) and Rick Thompson's problem, *The Leper* (V3).

The early 1980s started out strong with Rick and his partner, Scott Garso, adding *Wet Dreams* (11a) and *Ethereal Material* (12a) to the growing portfolio of Island Block desperates. Rick linked *The Traverse of The Swine* (V4) and I finished my projects *Birthday Boulder* (V5), *S.T.A.N.C.* (V4) and *Coup De Grace* (12a)—the latter involving some creative rope maneuvers to control the crater potential on the lower part of the route. About this time Chestnut Ridge and then the New River Gorge began exerting their magnetic influence on everyone, and the Mill became simply the place to go get pumped on a weekday evening. New route activity slowed to a crawl.

The 1990s have been a renaissance decade for the Mill. Prior to his relocating to Boulder, Rick Thompson had taken up residence within even closer striking distance to the park. He started the ball rolling with one of his parting shots, *She Got the Bosch* (12a), on the Island Block. The long standing aid eliminate *Crater Expectations* (11d) on Rappel Rock was done by Rick Zinnakas; local Chris Eckstein then added a new testpiece, *Hanging In Space* (12b), just to the right. An outbreak of the exploratory bug yielded a revisit to The Projects and soon

Bob Value on S.T.A.N.C.
Photo by Carl Samples.

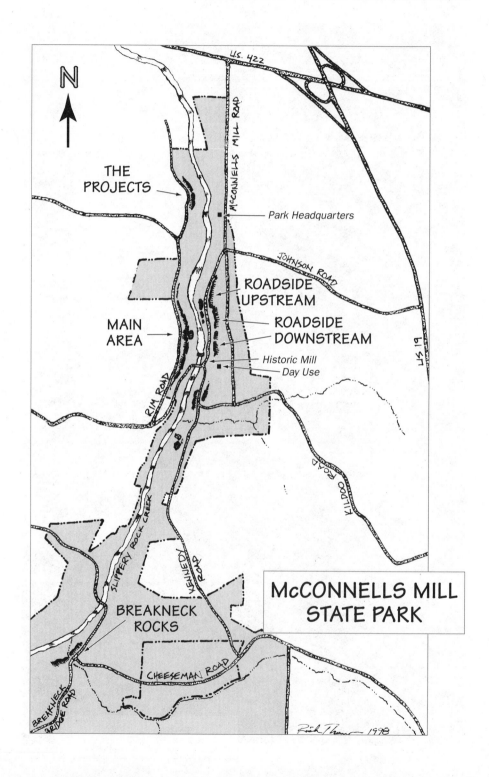

N

THE
PROJECTS

Park Headquarters

JOHNSON ROAD

ROADSIDE
UPSTREAM

MAIN
AREA

ROADSIDE
DOWNSTREAM

Historic Mill
Day Use

RIM ROAD

U.S. 422

McCONNELLS MILL ROAD

RT. 19

KILLDOO ROAD

BREAKNECK
ROCKS

SLIPPERY ROCK CREEK

KENNEDY ROAD

McCONNELLS MILL
STATE PARK

BREAKNECK
BRIDGE ROAD

CHEESEMAN ROAD

Rick Thorn 1998

the better Millstoned Wall routes were climbed. Crowded weekends at the Rim Road areas caused climbers to revisit the relatively secluded Breakneck Rocks, and several hard, thin face problems resulted.

On the bouldering scene, the remaining independent lines on Birthday Boulder were done, and several new problems and eliminates on the east face of the Island Block now exist. The most notable is Chris Eckstein's classic *Where's My Spot!* (V4 R). The sparsely pocketed wall left of *The Leper* finally yielded *The Burning Zone* (V6) after numerous attempts. Surprisingly, the Casino Boulder slumbered away a mere 100 feet from the most heavily climbed section of cliff until 1997, when several hours of brushing, as well as several long ground falls, yielded the "cool-headed" problem *Playing With A Full Deck* (V3 R).

While The Projects mark the end of the Rim Road areas covered in this guide, some isolated cliffs further upstream are starting to see exploration. For the enterprising rockhound there are climbing areas along the Slippery Rock watershed that are on private property (and outside the scope of this guide); these areas have only been partially explored. It is a good bet that the area has not given up all its secrets, and while new-route potential in the more accessible areas is maturing, there are certainly undiscovered classics waiting to be done.

USING THIS GUIDE This guide is arranged as logically as one might expect for an area that is comprised of jumbled blocks and long, unbroken walls. Written descriptions are often oriented relative to Slippery Rock Creek, which flows in a southerly direction—hence the upstream and downstream references. The Rim Road Areas are located on the west side of the creek while the Roadside and Breakneck Rocks are located on the east side of the creek. Climbs are listed in roughly the same order as they would be encountered if one were to explore the cliffs from the primary parking areas.

OVERVIEW MAPS An overview map of McConnells Mill State Park is included in this guide. It shows significant park features and climbing areas. This map will orient you to parking and access trails, and it will get you pointed toward your goals for the day. Additionally, there is an overview map for the entire Main Area along Rim Road.

What follows is a description of the overview maps to each specific area.

Rim Road: Main Area Upstream This map encompasses the area first encountered when starting from the picnic table along Rim Road. This area features Rappel Rock, Sunshine Wall, Ross Boulder, Casino Boulder, Ships Prow, and Beginners' Face.

Rim Road: Main Area Downstream Moving downstream on the trail below the cliffs, this map covers Island Block, Five Fingers Face and the corridors surrounding these primary features as well as Fall Safe Point and Birthday

Boulder. Beyond Birthday Boulder the cliffs begin to break down; there are some very noteworthy routes downstream (The Garden of Worldly Delights block comes to mind immediately), but they are spread out and are not included on the maps.

The Projects The final area along Rim Road covered in this guide, this area includes the Millstoned Wall, Beavis and Buttress and EuroChoss Wall. These areas are located further upstream from the Main Area along Rim Road.

Roadside: Upstream Area (closed to climbing) Encompasses the Roadside cliffs from the Johnson Road parking area downstream to Tarzan Wall, Son of Foops Block and Sunnyside Slab.

Roadside: Downstream Area (closed to climbing) This section continues the Roadside cliff coverage from *The Leper* downstream to the stairs above the mill.

The Blackboard (closed to climbing) and Traverse of The Swine Roadside cliffs downstream from the mill near the Kildoo Road & McConnells Mill Road intersection and the Traverse of The Swine block.

The Ecksandstein Routes in this little-known area are located even further downstream from the mill and encompass two blocks located on the uppermost fork of the foot trail running from the mill downstream to Breakneck Bridge.

Breakneck This area encompasses the two walls immediately upstream and downstream from Breakneck Falls. The upstream (or North Wall) starts at the base of the steep descent path and continues downstream to the falls. The downstream (or South Wall) routes continue from the falls along the cliff to the point where the cliff becomes increasingly broken and no longer parallels Cheeseman Run.

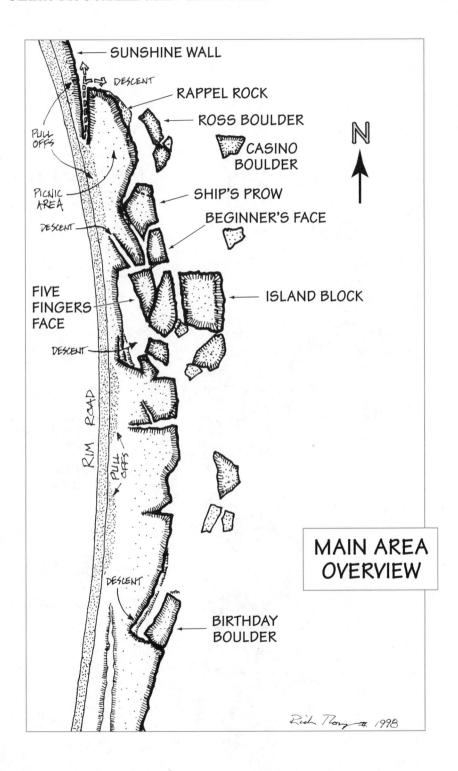

SUNSHINE WALL

DESCENT

RAPPEL ROCK

ROSS BOULDER

PULL OFFS

CASINO BOULDER

N

PICNIC AREA

SHIP'S PROW

DESCENT

BEGINNER'S FACE

FIVE FINGERS FACE

ISLAND BLOCK

DESCENT

RIM ROAD

PULL OFFS

DESCENT

MAIN AREA OVERVIEW

BIRTHDAY BOULDER

Rich Thorn 1998

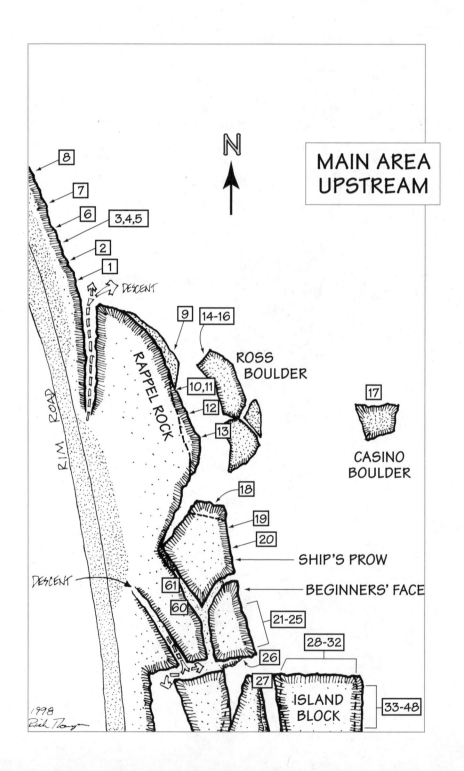

CHAPTER ONE

Rim Road Area

To reach the Rim Road climbing areas follow signs in the park to the mill. At the mill bear left and go across the covered bridge. At the top of the hill turn right on the dirt road. This is Rim Road. Follow the road upstream about 0.4 mile until you see the picnic table and large flat area. This is the normal parking area for the climbs located in the Main Area. Descent is through the large crevasse on the upstream side of this flat area.

MAIN AREA: UPSTREAM

Sunshine Wall (aka The Windowpane)

At the base of the descent crevasse the cliff extends upstream and forms a clean (by Mill standards) face.

1   **Schmeggie (10a)** Just beyond the entrance to the crevasse, climb the short flake system through vertical mud to the top. Not recommended.

2   **Welcome to The Mill (12a/b)** ★ Starting just right of *Schmeggie*, climb up a line of tenuous crimps, finishing just left of the *Sunshine* topout. Originally a hard alternative boulder start to *Sunshine*, the complete route, while squeezed, does remain independent of its neighbors. FA: Bob Value, 1995.

3   **Sunshine (9+)** ★★★ About 20 feet upstream from the crevasse is a prominent line up the relatively clean, white face. Originally this route, like many in the park, required significant scrubbing. Unlike its less popular neighbors, the constant traffic on this classic keeps it in relatively good shape. Using either of two bouldery starts, move up, aiming for the shallow right-facing corner. Finish at the tree.

4   **Windowpain (V3)** Start on *Sunshine* and traverse right as for *Green Microdots*, then continue up and right to finish on Route 6.

5   **Green Microdots (12a)** Start on *Sunshine*. Make a low traverse right for several moves and then climb straight up the face on small crimpers to finish at the dwarf pine. As of 1997 the route needed scrubbing; however, the quality of the climbing does not justify the environmental impact. FA: Bob Value, 1983.

6   Unnamed (7) Twenty feet right of *Sunshine* is a series of deep but dirty horizontal pockets leading to the top.

7   Mr. Clean (10c) ★★★ Right of Route 6 is another clean-looking white face. Starting below the small roof, pull up and onto the clean face and follow the center of it straight to the top. Stepping right to slightly larger holds makes the route several letter grades easier. FA: Bob Value, 1974.

8   Unnamed (7/8) ★ Ten yards upstream and around the corner is another semi-clean face. After a broken start, fun face climbing leads to the top.

Above and to the right of Route 8 a series of ledges leads to the top. On the right side of the top tier of this system is a boulder that offers about a half-dozen moderate problems. In the mid-1970s Don French and Tim Campbell reported climbing a moderate overhang in this section of cliff which is possibly the short roof and crack just right of Route 8. No other information is available on this route.

Rappel Rock (aka R.O.T.C. Wall aka H&R Block)

By following the path down the crevasse and bearing right at the bottom of the cliff, you pass under an overhanging wall broken by a ledge on its right side. The area of cliff from the large fissure at the left side of this wall upstream to the descent crevasse is known by many names, most popularly Rappel Rock, R.O.T.C. Wall, and H&R Block. If you question the first two names, look for the highest concentration of sport rappellers plunging face-first, Aussie-style down the cliff.

9   Boulder Dash (V0+ R) Start to the right of the left-leaning crack, in the back of the alcove formed between the face and the large boulder; surmount the roof and pull onto the face above. Bad landing. FA: Jack Nard, 1977.

10   R.O.T.C. Route (7/8) ★★ Climb the obvious chimney (easiest), the face, or the left-leaning crack system to the large ledge. Follow the face up to the top or climb up and left to meet *Laid Back* at its last move.

11   Laid Back (10b) ★★★ Follow the left-leaning crack system up and left, avoiding the large ledge. Step left and follow the steep face and flake to the top. FA: Bob Value, 1973.

12   Hanging in Space (12b) ★★ Start at the small right-facing flake off the right edge of the same boulder as *Crater Expectations*. Power over a short steep bulge to gain an awkward stance at the base of the overhanging wall between *Laid Back* and *Crater Expectations*. Climb up and then move left, aiming for the notch on the right side of the large triangular roof. Pull the notch and traverse back right across the tier. Finish up the final short face. A fall from the first crux down low will result in a groundfall if a backrope is not used. FA: Chris Eckstein, 1995.

13   **Crater Expectations (11d)** ★★★ Beware! The name speaks for itself. This is an old aid line that is now a fun testpiece with multiple cruxes. The climb is located below the large triangular roof. Start at the piton-scarred flake on the left side of the large boulder. Climb awkward, powerful moves through the first bulge. Move out left and pull through a thin move at the nose of the second bulge and continue up to the large ledge. Get a shake and move up and right through the final bulge to the top. An additional hard move can be added by starting off the ground. FFA: Rick "Zinc" Zinnakas, 1994.

Ross Boulder

Directly behind Laid Back a series of three short blocks forms a long, low wall. The block on the upstream side is Ross Boulder. Many variations and eliminates exist in addition to those listed.

14   **Ross's Boulder (V0+)** ★★ Stay just left of the right arête of the boulder; follow pockets and edges to the top. This was once the bouldering testpiece in the park, and the opening moves still spit off many attempts. FA: Nick Ross, early 1970s.

14a   **Variation (V2)** ★ Eliminates the right arête and the holds on the *Center Route.* FA: Bill Crick, 1976.

14b   **Variation: Sit Down Start (V4)** ★★ Start at the two low pockets below the arête. Dry conditions are helpful for the initial slaps up the bottom of the arête. FA: Bob Value, 1983.

15   **Short Traverse (V1)** ★ Traversing either direction on Ross Boulder is fun but starting on the right side, moving left and then finishing up the sloping left edge of the block offers the best line. FA: Bill Crick, 1974.

15a   **Variation: Long Traverse (V2)** Start on the far-right block, traverse left without using the top edges of any blocks to join and finish on *The Short Traverse.* FA: Bob Value, 1975.

16   **Center Route (V0)** ★★ Climb the obvious flake and horizontals in the center of Ross Boulder to the top.

Casino Boulder

To find Casino Boulder, follow the trail downhill behind Ross Boulder for about 100 feet. Here you will be rewarded with a 20-foot high steep, thin slab. This is Casino Boulder.

17   **Playing with a Full Deck (V3 R or 11d/12a)** ★★ Climb the center of the slab using freaky sidepulls and crimps. The crux is the last 1/3 of the route. Most would-be boulderers have felt the need to "test the waters" via the long

jump before committing to the crux series of moves. If you are not feeling lucky, the route is an enjoyable toprope with easy rigging. FA: Bob Value, 1997.

Ship's Prow & Beginners' Face

This face has slowly outgrown its name over the years as more difficult variations have been established. However, the original Beginners' Face route still sees its share of novice ascents. To get to Beginners' Face, follow the under-cliff trail downstream past Rappel Rock, then past the large fissure, and then around the corner. You should be at the base of a long, slabby face broken by a short chimney (an alternative access point). The wall to the left of the chimney is named Beginners' Face; the block to the right of the chimney is dubbed Ship's Prow.

18   Mini Ovest aka Peter Pan (11d) ★★★ Younger climbers may not know that this route name is a pun of a famous Dolomite big wall, the Cima Ovest, which features a huge, intimidating roof. The cliff forms the left side of a deep fissure around the right side of the Ship's Prow. Start near the left side of this overhanging prow. About 15 feet up move right to the edge of the prow and then continue up steep rock, traversing up and back left. The crux is encountered at the final overhang. It is also possible to start by climbing straight up the right side. **NOTE:** Use a backrope on this climb. A fall from either variation (5.9) would most likely result in a groundfall or a wild swing into a neighboring boulder if a backrope is not used. In late 1996 a key crux hold broke, slightly increasing the difficulty. This climb was visionary (by Mill standards) at the time it was originally done. FA: Eric Guerrin, 1979.

18a   Variation: Tinker Belle (10d/11a) ★ Start on the left side of prow, but instead of moving right into the main overhangs in a manly fashion, continue up the arête on jugs. Finish at the small tree 10 feet below the final roof on *Mini-Ovest*.

19   All Hands or Deck (9) Follow the blunt arête on the right side of the Ship's Prow, just around the corner from *Tinker Belle* to the top. FA: Bob Value, 1974.

20   You Name It (5) ★★ Everyone seems to have a different name for this route. Midway between the chimney and the right edge of the Ship's Prow is a line of weakness leading up the slabby face, over a small roof, and finishing up on an exit slab. A classic Mill moderate that offers a — you name it — variety of moves.

BOULDER NOTE: *A couple of moderate boulder problems, along with a very difficult dynamic problem pioneered by Shawn McGuirk, exist on the right side of the chimney that splits the face.*

Chris Eckstein on Where's My Spot!
Photo by Carl Samples.

21   Squids in Bondage (10a) ★ From the obvious flake and pockets 10 feet left of the chimney that splits the face, climb up and over the bulges to a ledge. Finish up and right of the standard *Beginners' Face* route. "Squid" was a term coined in the mid-1970s by Don French. It refers to beginning climbers — they often climb using all arms and no feet.

22   The Fast Track (10a) ★ This is a direct start to *Beginners' Face*. Climb the face and left-facing flakes up to and over a bulge 10 feet right of *Beginners' Face*. At the ledge, continue up to finish on the standard route. FA: Bob Broughton, 1971.

23   Beginners' Face (4) ★ Climb the line of least resistance just right of the arête to the ledge and then to the top.

24   Sink or Swim Traverse (V3) ★ Traverse low across the entire *Beginners' Face* from the chimney on the right to the left arête. The crux comes as you move through the smooth section of rock in the center of the face.

25   Beginners Lament (8) ★ Climb directly up the arête that forms the left edge of the *Beginners' Face*.

26   Beginners Beware (10b/c) ★ Located in the chimney around the left corner from the actual *Beginners' Face*. Climb directly up the center of the face without using the back wall. A stretchy rope or inattentive belay at the crux could make your chiropractor a rich man. FA: Bob Value, 1975.

Island Block: North Face

Directly kitty-corner from the Beginners' Face route is an enormous floating block, home to some of the best routes and boulder problems at the Mill. The Island Block offers a respite to climbers seeking sanctuary from sport rappellers. To arrange topropes, solo the southwest corner, named the Rigging Route. CAUTION: This is a scary, 20-foot (or more) solo on sloping holds with a bad landing. This corner has been the scene of several bad accidents and becomes even more dangerous if it is wet. Please exercise extreme caution here; additional accidents could jeopardize access to this block and the entire park. In addition, climbers should tread lightly when moving about the top of the block; it is suffering from severe soil compaction. This compaction and the accompanying wear and tear from rigging anchors has already jeopardized trees and ground vegetation.

27   The Arête (7+) ★★★ Located on the right side of the north face of the block, directly across from *Beginners' Face*. Climb the overhanging arête through bulges and then balance your way up the slab to the top. An early classic. Anchor chains have been installed on the belay tree at the top in an attempt to protect it from further damage. As of 1998 they were still there. Please do not remove or tamper with this fixed anchor.

28   Temptation (11a) ★★ Possibly the first 5.11 in the park. Climb the short bulge and clean face 5 feet left of *The Arête*, resisting the urge to move right and use the arête. FA: Bob Value, 1976.

28a   Variation (11b) ★ Wander up the face between *Temptation* and *Mission Impossible*, trying to maintain an independent line.

29   Mission Impossible aka Impossible Dreams (10d) ★★★ This is the classic face climb on this block! Begin by following the right-angling line of weakness in the center of the face to a stance below the small roof. Pull the roof to another small stance. Climb up and right through a series of artful moves and then finish back left, topping out just right of the mossy groove. This route is considered an entry exam all climbers must pass before moving on to try the harder routes in the park. You can count on waiting in line most weekends. FA: Rick Thompson, 1977.

29a   Variation: Cruise This Tom (11a/b) ★★ Fire straight up from the small stance above the roof on *Mission Impossible* through a series of slopers to meet the regular route at its finish.

30   Ethereal Material (12a) ★★ Most likely the first 5.12 in the park. Although somewhat contrived, this line nonetheless offers a series of thoughtful, technical cruxes. Start in the center of the face and climb directly over a bulge to a stance. Make a fingery traverse right, then move up a few moves. Step left and then climb directly up the left side of the blunt prow. FA: Rick Thompson, 1980.

31   Wet Dreams (11a) ★★ Using the same start as *Ethereal Material*, pull the bulge and move up and left to a stance. Climb directly up a few moves, then up and right, eventually finishing straight up the face. FA: Scott Garso, 1980.

31a   Variation (10d) ★ From the stance above the first bulge on *Wet Dreams*, climb up and to the left of the normal route.

32   Rude Awakening (11b/c) Climb the weakness on the left side of the wall to a sloping ledge. Follow the arête to the top. FA: Rick Zinnakas, 1989.

Island Block: East Face

The east face of Island Block is home to a number of excellent boulder problems. So far only one confirmed route tops out. The wall is sheltered from rain but will suffer from seepage after a prolonged storm. Many of these boulders feature long moves that may be height-dependent. This is a very good wall to help get your open-hand strength in order. While the boulder problems are not technically considered "high" problems, they seem high enough when you consider that the years of heavy foot traffic at the base have compacted the landing zones into a concrete-like consistency. Most problems end at a horizontal band about

15 feet off the ground; descent is accomplished either by down-climbing your selected problem or jumping off. A crash pad will go a long way to help eliminate bruised heels and twisted ankles. Once again, this guide is not a replacement for individual judgment and discretion in choosing appropriate problems. Routes are listed from right to left.

33   **Liquid Lunger (V2)** Start just left of the corner and make dynamic moves up to an awkward mantle on the sloping ledge. Can be used as a direct start to Route 32. FA: Bill Crick, 1977.

34   **Project** The low traverse of the entire east face has been a long standing project that at press time had not received a confirmed ascent.

35   **Smell the Glove (V3)** ★★ Begin at the obvious triangular hole and the two finger pocket 10 feet left of the corner. Power up and over the bulge off of the pocket and continue up to the sloping ledge. Jump or make a scary mantle onto the sloping ledge. You need to top out via the mantle at least once to get the tick. FA: Bob Value, 1977.

36   **Le Menestral Crimps (V3/V4)** Starting three feet left of *Smell the Glove*, crimp up to the horizontal band below the short bulge and traverse right to a long finish at a hold just left and above the sloping ledge at the end of *Smell the Glove*. FA: Bob Value, 1997.

37   **Where's My Spot! (V4? R)** ★★★ Start on *Le Menestral Crimps*, but continue straight up over the bulge at the horizontal band via the shallow monodoight and a wild leap of faith. Find your spot on the dyno or hope that your spot finds you on the express ride down! This is the park's current "high hard one." It is hard to judge the technical grade of this problem as the crux move is intimidating. FA: Chris Eckstein, 1996.

38   **American Spurtsman (V4)** ★★ Begins just left of *Where's My Spot* and directly above the chiseled name "Tom Miller," at a series of square-cut flakes and slopers. Crimp and slap up and then left to a very long finishing move at the in situ birds' nest in the obvious horizontal band. The last move on this problem is height-dependent and sees more "big air" than any other problem in the park.

39   **Unnamed (V4/V5)** ★★ Start just left of *American Spurtsman* on sloping holds and move up and then right to the hand match that sets up the finishing move on *American Spurtsman*. FA: Chris Eckstein, 1996.

40   **Snake Bit (V2)** ★★ Just right of the obvious line of buckets in the center of the wall are several letterbox horizontals that lead to a long blank stretch before reaching more pockets. Dyno or make a long lock off to either of the two upper pockets and continue up to the horizontal band. If you miss the dyno, the crystal in the upper-right pocket may leave your finger looking snakebitten. Several variations are possible. FA: Bob Value, 1978.

40a Shawn's Eliminate (V5) This is a six-foot all-points dyno. Set up off the letterbox on *Snakebit* and launch all the way to the horizontal band. FA: Shawn McGuirk, 1997.

41 Doc Says You're Gonna Die aka Chin and Bear It (V0+) This was the first of the Island Block boulders to go. Climb the obvious buckets in the center of the wall, move through an awkward mantel, and then continue up to the horizontal band.

42 Wonder World (V4) ★★ Just left of *Chin and Bear It* (and three feet right of the chiseled initials "CN") a series of pockets starts at waist level and leads to a deceptive move over a blank bulge. Beta on the crafty crux move will cost you a grade. FA: Chris Eckstein, 1995.

43 Cold Day In Hell aka The Flying Nun (V3) ★ Start 5 feet right of *S.T.A.N.C.* and 2 feet left of the chiseled initials "CN" at good pockets over the "swamp." Climb up to a long move over the bulge and go for the horizontal band. FA: Chris Eckstein, 1997.

44 S.T.A.N.C. aka Mr. Smoothie (V4) ★★★ A powerful open-hand problem. Just right of the shallow right-facing corner is a series of smooth, sloping holds separated by long reaches. Using either of two starts, follow the slopers to the horizontal band. FA: Bob Value, 1980.

45 Smooth Extension (V4) Start between *S.T.A.N.C.* and *Spurtin Outcomes*. Move up and right to *S.T.A.N.C.* and then finish back left of the normal *S.T.A.N.C.* finish at the incut hold at the top of the *Spurtin Outcomes*. FA: Chris Eckstein, 1995.

46 Spurtin Outcomes (V1) ★ There are numerous variations up this shallow right-facing corner as well as on the face just left of it that is located above the chiseled initials "BG" and "RH."

47 She Got the Bosch, I Got Drilled (12a) ★★ Divorce can be costly! Start 10 feet left of the shallow corner, approximately 3 feet left of the chiseled initials "WS 60." Awkward moves lead up and right to a series of bulges. Pull through the bulges, past a notoriously damp pocket, and head up the right-angling flake to the top. Beware: This is yet another of those very overhung climbs where failure on the first third of the route could be costly. Use a backrope. FA: Rick Thompson, 1992.

48 Prenuptial Taste Test (V0) Climb the dripping buckets on the far-left side of the wall as high as you dare.

Around the corner from Prenuptial Taste Test you pass under a tunnel formed by a large, detached block leaning against the Island Block.

49   The Good, The Bad, and The Ugly (9-10) ★ There are three short toprope variations that are known to exist on the overhanging southwest face of the small block.

Island Block: West Face

Continuing around the Island Block one will see the southwest corner, known as the Rigging Route, which is the recommended access route to rig and de-rig climbs on the block. Both high and low boulder problem traverses exist across the entire west face (VO R). The landing is poor in places.

50   Rigging Route (4) Exercising great care, make balancy moves up the sloping southwest corner of Island Block.

51   Unnamed (8) ★ Ten feet left of *Rigging Route* is a short bulge leading to a low-angled slabby face.

52   Lean Across (6) ★★ Midway on the west face, at the point where the overhang is widest, lean across the chasm from the neighboring ledge. Swing over the roof and follow the face to the top. There are three or four variation starts and at least as many finishes to this route. The hardest variation starts off the ground and takes the roof directly at its wide point (10).

53   Unnamed (9) ★ Starting 10 feet left of *Lean Across* at an obvious line of weakness. Follow positive holds over the bulge and up the face to the top.

MAIN AREA: DOWNSTREAM

Five Fingers Block

From the parking area and picnic table walk about 60 feet downstream on Rim Road. The Five Fingers Block will be visible on your left. If you are at the bottom of the cliffs, the block can best be reached by walking through the corridor located on the left side of Beginners' Face. Either make a short scramble up the ledge system on the right (this will deposit you near the north face) or walk left through the tunnel which leads to the right edge of the west face.

This short block offers face climbs at all levels of difficulty and is one of the first faces to see the spring thaw. The block forms a rough equilateral triangle. The southeast wall forms a tunnel. It is extremely overhung and never sees the light of day. There are several boulder problems here, but they all have exceptionally dangerous landings. The routes listed start on the left side of the north face and move left-to-right around and onto the west wall. Numerous variations exist on the west face; the following lines are suggestions only.

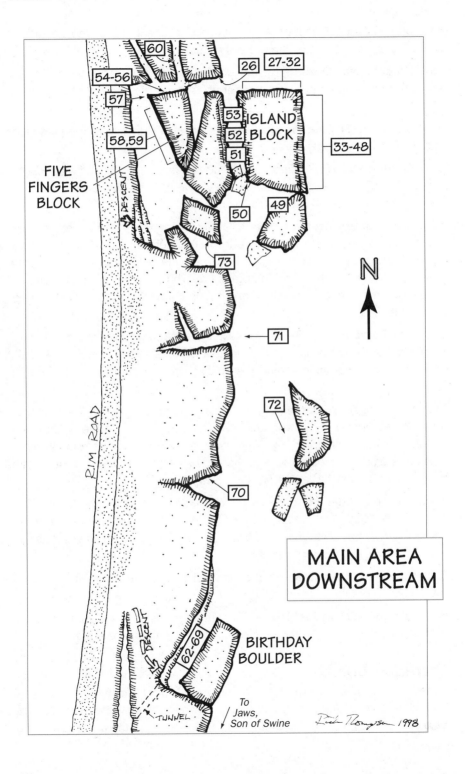

54   **Stupid Crack (1)** Start where the trail at the base of the north face climbs over a short hump; climb the short ugly crack to the top of the wall.

55   **Primeheaval Ooze (8)** In the center of the moss-covered north face start on good holds and move straight up through the vertical swamp to the top.

55a   **Variation (8)** After the initial moves, traverse right across the entire face and finish up *Five Fingers Arête.*

56   **Garden Club (8)** Climb straight up the face 7 feet left of *Five Fingers Arête.* Though cleaner than *Primeheaval Ooze,* the greasy slopers at the top detract from what could be fun climbing.

57   **Five Fingers Arête (8)** ★★★ Classic! Gymnastic opening moves give way to a subtle sequence up the left edge of the arête, or you can stay right and keep grunting. The opening moves have become quite a bit easier over the years due to the fact that erosion from the nearby bank has raised the ground level more than two feet since the early 1970s. Even so, there is often a cheater block at the start of the route.

58   **Five Fingers Face (5 - 11)** ★★ Just about every inch of the west face has been climbed, with the harder variations being located to the immediate right and left of the tree leaning against the wall. The easier routes are near the right edge of the wall.

59   **Five Fingers Traverse (V3)** ★★ Start on the right edge of the west face, traverse left across the lower face—avoiding the small ledge system that develops—and finish up on *Five Fingers Arête.* A great stamina route to pump laps on. The crux moves come near the end of the traverse, and a fall from here might result in a twisted ankle. FA: Bill Crick, 1978.

Routes 60 and 61 can be found by starting under the north face of the block, following the trail east (under Stupid Crack) to the point where it becomes necessary to down climb the short ledge system. Walk through the cleft on your left.

60   **Unnamed (6)** Midway on the left wall that forms the cleft is a short, broken, hand crack. Follow it to the top.

61   **Unnamed (7)** At the end of the cleft is an off-sized crack in an inside corner. Finesse the crack and then grunt over the small roof at the top.

Birthday Boulder

The slightly overhanging west face of Birthday Boulder offers some of the best crimp problems in the park. At one time some vandals sprayed this face with graffiti, specifically "Happy Birthday Bob," which is where the name came from.

From the turnoff follow Rim Road for 0.2 mile. Watch for a parking pullover with a triangular point of rock visible over the main cliff face. If traveling on foot from the picnic area, follow the under-cliff trail around the east face of Island Block; go through the tunnel and bear left. Follow the bottom of the main cliff for approximately 150 yards (going past Routes 70-73). The climbs on Birthday Boulder are listed left to right. There are actually eight independent lines; the remainder are extensions and variations.

62   Jail Bait (V0-) Climb awkward moves up the left arête. FA: Bob Value, 1972.

63   Middle Edge (V3) ★ Climb sharp edges 5 feet right of the arête. FA: Bob Value, 1992.

63a   Variation: Old and in the Way (V4) Start on *Jail Bait* and move up and right to the shallow pocket on Birthday Boulder. FA: Bob Value, 1996.

64   Birthday Boulder (V5) ★★★ This problem is historically significant because for many years it was the hardest problem in the park and was probably the first V5 in western Pennsylvania. Begin at the obvious, deep letterbox in the center of the face. Climb up to the letterbox, through the shallow finger pocket and small edge to the top. FA: Bob Value, 1981.

Kurt Byrnes on Birthday Boulder.
Photo by Carl Samples.

65   The Cutting Edge (V4 R) ★★★ A more sustained companion route to *Birthday Boulder* though it has no "stopper move." Start below the two finger pocket located 5 feet right of *Birthday Boulder.* Climb the crimpfest between *Birthday Boulder* and *Sweet Dreams.* A harder version eliminates the use of the letterbox on the left as a foothold. The route is named in honor of the notorious, sharp-as-a-guillotine lip of the one finger pocket. This sharp lip shattered on a later ascent. Poor landing. FA: Bob Value, 1996.

66   Sweet Dreams (V0+ R) ★★★ Superb moves up the gently overhanging wall on small but very positive holds make this the classic boulder problem for its grade in the park. Climb the small, incut edges up the right side of the face. Make an awkward mantel at the top. Poor landing. FA: Bob Value, 1973.

67   New Edge (V3/V4) ★★ Start on *Jail Bait* and traverse right across the entire lower face and finish up *Sweet Dreams.* FA: Chris Eckstein, 1996.

67a Variation: Edge of Consent (V3/V4) Start on *Jail Bait*, traverse right to the letterbox on *Birthday Boulder.* Move up and right to link with *Cutting Edge* at its final small crimper. FA: Bob Value, 1996.

67b Variation: The Party's Over (V5) ★★ A link-up. Start on *Jail Bait* and traverse right. Finish up *Birthday Boulder.* FA: Bob Value, 1996.

67c Variation: Toast Master (V5) ★★ A link-up. Start on *Jail Bait*, traverse right to finish on the regular *Cutting Edge.* FA: Bob Value, 1996.

68   Cakewalk (V0+ R) Sit-down start. Climb sharp edges to the right arête; don't use the neighboring block. Poor landing. FA: Bob Value, 1975.

69   Feeling My Edge (V4) ★★ Start on *Cakewalk* and traverse left across the face to finish on *Jail Bait.* Routes 69a, 69b, and 69c are all variations of this problem. FA: All variations Bob Value, 1997.

69a Variation: Link to Middle Edge (V4) ★

69b Variation: Link to Cutting Edge (V4/V5) ★★

69c Variation: Link to Birthday Boulder (V5/V6) ★★

Miscellaneous

The following noteworthy climbs and boulders are spread out in the numerous rock cities that exist between Island Block and the downstream terminus of the cliffs. Approaches are described from Birthday Boulder.

From Birthday Boulder, squirm downstream through the tunnel. The first block on your left has several moderate boulder problems on its west face. Next, a large floating block appears on your left. This block is known as The Garden of Worldly

Delights. The west face of this block has four very fun routes, all (9) to (10) in difficulty, that were first ascended in the mid-1970s. This block also offers a difficult low traverse and several high boulder problems. There is an often-wet boulder problem located under the tunnel on the north side (Anonymous Bosch V0), as well as an overhanging traverse and a crack (sit-down start) on the south wall. This is a nice, quiet climbing area when the upstream cliffs seem too crowded.

Jaws (V0+) Downstream, just beyond *The Garden of Worldly Delights*, is another small block which has a fun traverse on its gritty, bucketed north face. Another problem (*Rasp* V1) ascends the left arete of the north face using a sitdown start.

Son of Swine (V0-V2) ★ Continue downstream along the trail from *Jaws* and eventually you will cross a small, seeping spring. Beyond this seep 100 feet, to the left of the path, is a short attractive boulder with a pocketed west face. It is possible, through various eliminates, to do the traverse of this face.

There are also some routes scattered between Island Block and Birthday Boulder. They begin approximately 100 feet upstream (north) from Birthday Boulder, at a point where the cliff turns west to form a crevasse. There is a small section of cliff here that offers some moderate, entertaining boulders.

70   Unnamed (4) Located 100 feet upstream (north) from Birthday Boulder. Climb the center of the southeast-facing slab.

71   Flap Jack (V0-V1) ★ Just north of the slab the cliff is broken by a crevasse (an alternative access point). The overhang on the north corner of this crevasse yields many fun boulder and toprope variations up to V1 in difficulty. The overhang and arête itself goes at 5.10. **NOTE:** Extreme caution should be exercised while using the large flake (known as The Pancake) at the lip of the roof. It moves when weighted.

72   Fall Safe Point (V0+ R) ★ Once you're past the "fall safe point" there is no turning back. From *Flap Jack*, behind you toward the river, is a block with a large, triangular point. This is known as Fall Safe Point. Boulder straight up and over the overhanging point and make a scary mantel to get on top. Poor landing. FA: Bob Value, 1980.

73   Unnamed (9) Located back on the main cliffband, midway between the *Flap Jack* arête and Island Block. This is another crevasse with yet another overhanging arête. There are several variations on the face to the left of the arête, all of which are now overgrown.

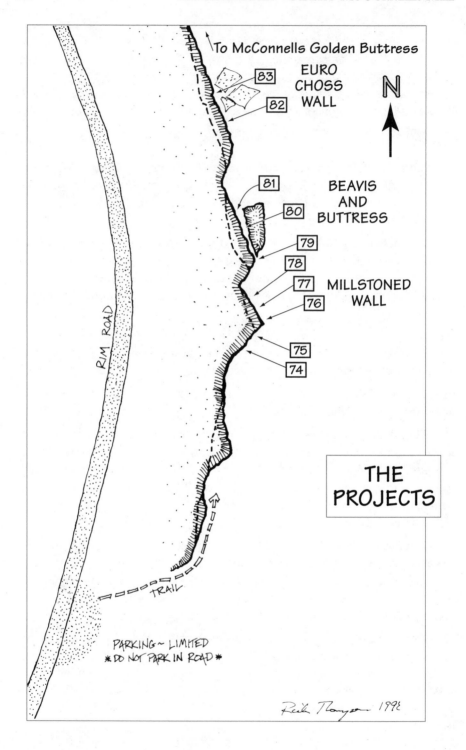

To McConnells Golden Buttress

EURO
CHOSS
WALL

83

82

N

81

80

BEAVIS
AND
BUTTRESS

79

78

77

76

MILLSTONED
WALL

75

74

RIM ROAD

THE
PROJECTS

TRAIL

PARKING ~ LIMITED
* DO NOT PARK IN ROAD *

Rick Thompson 1998

THE PROJECTS

To reach The Projects, continue driving up Rim Road beyond the Main Area. At the fork in the road go right for about 200 feet. On your right will be a small dirt pullover. Follow the trail from the pullover down the steep bank and then upstream. About 50 yards along the cliff is an overhanging arête with a nice looking slab on the left side. This is Millstoned Wall.

NOTE: Until you become familiar with the area, it is a good idea to have someone at the base of the cliff guide the person setting up the topropes.

The routes and formations in The Projects are described from south to north.

Millstoned Wall

In the spring of 1994, Rick Thompson and I were walking the cliffs in search of fresh rock. We decided to head upstream to an area we hadn't visited for years. Suffering from both eternal optimism and long-term memory loss, I joked that western Pennsylvania's answer to the New River Gorge's classic steep route *Lactic Acid Bath*, was probably lying just around the corner, waiting to be climbed. Lo and behold—there it was. And while not as grand as the real *Lactic Acid Bath*, this crag offers some of the best overhanging routes to be found at the Mill.

74   Bran Flake aka Where the Sun Never Shines (9) ★ (At the Mill, that is!) Start on the left side of the arête and climb the face to gain a short right-facing corner. At the small ledge at the top of the corner, move onto the slab and continue to the top. FA: Ron Kampas, 1994.

75   Swillstoned aka Journey to Uranus (11b/c) ★ Start on the arête and climb straight up, taking care not to use the neighboring corner. Make a thin move to gain the slab and finish either straight up or traverse right and back left to the top. Contrived route, but the moves are good. FA: Bob Value, 1994.

76   Fine Grind (11c/d) ★★★ Around the arête there is an obvious finger crack leading to the right edge of a large roof. Follow the crack to the roof, step right and up into the huecos. Immediately above the roof make a strenuous rail back left and follow the right side of the arête to the top. Height dependant crux. One of the better lines in the park for its grade. FA: Bob Value, 1994.

76a Variation: Nose to the Grindstone (11d) ★★★ At the top of the crack step left and pull the roof to join the regular route at its crux. FA: Bob Value, 1994.

76b Variation: Stoneground (11a/b) ★ Midway across the traverse make a powerful move up the bulge staying just right of the normal route to the top. FA: Rick Thompson, 1994.

76c Variation: Millstoned (10b) ★★★ At the point where the regular route traverses left across the lip of the roof, continue straight up through the overhanging huecos. FA: Rick Thompson, 1994

Mark Van Cura on Fine Grind.
Photo by Carl Samples.

77   The Daily Grind (10a) ★ Both this and *Millstoned* are fine training routes to run endurance laps on. Follow the line of flakes and pockets to the right of *Fine Grind*, being careful of the large hollow flake at the bottom.

78   True Grits aka This Wall Needs an Enema (10b/c) On the right side of Millstoned Wall is a short, shallow corner. Follow the corner and face to the short, bulging wall at the top.

78a   Variation: Grits and Greens aka Urine Trouble Now (10c/d) At the shallow corner move left 3 feet and then pull through the crescent arch. Finish up the short, vegetated face.

Beavis and Buttress

The next buttress upstream (north) from the Millstoned Wall features another overhanging arête known as Beavis and Buttress

79   Project: The Great Cornholeo Starting at (on) the large (tonnage involved) chockstone, surmount the large finger-pocketed roof at the start of the arête. Power up the right side of the arête above the roof.

80   Project: Leave It To Beavis Features an easier start 10 feet right of arête. Climb over bulge and then rail left to join *Cornholeo* at the arête.

81   Kick Me In The Jimmies (11d/12a) ★★ Start approximately 20 feet right of the arête; follow the face up to gain the obvious flake, then continue up the pocketed wall. FA: Rick Thompson, 1994.

The EuroChoss Wall

Approximately 50 yards further upstream is a long overhanging wall broken by a roof band at mid-height.

82   Way of the Carpenter (12d) ★★★ Just left of the obvious hanging corner located midway along the wall is a series of pocketed bulges with a line of fixed gear. Climb out the first roof at the large block. Make a hard move over the lip and move up and left, aiming for the small right-facing flake. Make another very hard move at the flake and continue up the overhanging headwall on shallow pockets. FA Chris Eckstein 1998.

83   Blame It on Rico (12a) ★ Midway along the wall is a body-length flake that goes out a horizontal roof leading up into an obvious, right-facing, overhanging corner and crack system. Climb through the chossy start and out the roof; follow the corner and crack to the top. Unfortunately, this route is not recommended in its present condition. Although the move at the lip of the roof and the corner above offer good, sustained climbing, a fall from the lower part of the route would result in decking-out onto boulders or taking a nasty swing into the trees. Also, the large flake in the roof is hollow-sounding in places.

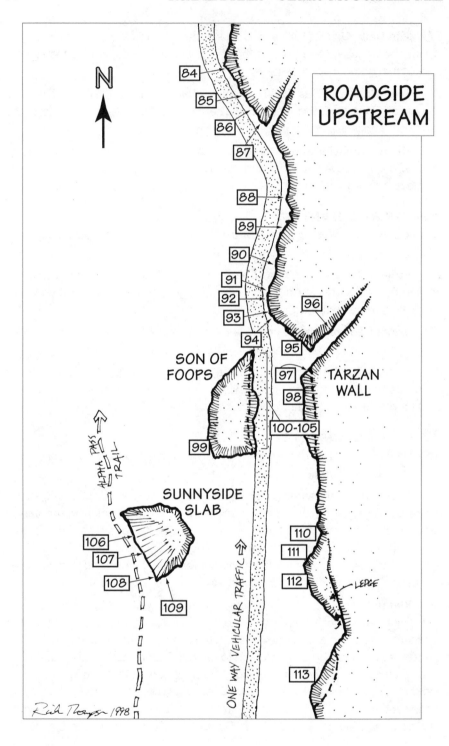

ROADSIDE
UPSTREAM

N

84
85
86
87
88
89
90
91
92
93
94
95
96

SON OF
FOOPS

TARZAN
WALL

97
98
100-105
99

ALPHA PASS
TRAIL

SUNNYSIDE
SLAB

106
107
108
109

ONE WAY VEHICULAR TRAFFIC

110
111
112
113

LEDGE

Rich Thompson 1998

CHAPTER TWO

Roadside Area

IMPORTANT NOTE: As stated at the beginning of this guide, climbing is forbidden anywhere along the road. These routes are included only for historical reasons and in the hope that someday they will be reopened for bouldering and some limited climbing. Roadside climbs tend to be warmer and dryer than most of the crags in the park. Unfortunately, they also happen to start right on the most traveled section of road in the park—that's why the authorities have closed them to climbing.

The Roadside Area encompasses the cliffs between Kildoo Road to the south (upstream) to the upper parking lot at the McConnells Mill Road/Johnson Road intersection to the north. This is the recommended parking area for those wishing to walk this section of cliff.

UPSTREAM

Tarzan/Son of Foops Area

84   **Tales of Powder (V2)** ★ "Chalk" up another Mill roof problem. The first large overhang found on the left side of the road when walking along the cliff from the parking lot. Begins at the widest point where the roof overhangs the road. Start in the center of this roof and climb out the obvious flake system; finish just below the dirty ledge. FA: Jack Nard, 1980.

85   **Primo Teen Miss (V3)** ★★ Climb dynamic, crimpy moves straight up to the notch to join *Hack Hard*. FA: Glenn Thomas, 1981.

86   **Hack Hard (V2/V3)** ★ Start on *Short Man's Problem*, then hand traverse left some 15 feet along the edge of the roof. At the notch move up and left, finishing at an obvious bucket just below the dirty ledge. FA: Jack Nard, 1980.

87   **Short Man's Problem aka It's Not the Size, It's the Motion (V2)** ★★ Just left of the brown streak is a deep chimney/gully. Pinch and crimp your way up the arête on the outside edge of the left wall. FA: Bill Crick, 1975.

88   Black Jack (V2) Located 30 feet downstream from the chimney/gully. The cliff is marked by a 20-foot wide dark streak. Start on the right edge of the wall and traverse left across the streak at the obvious horizontal band. Usually wet. FA: Jack Nard, 1980.

89   Roads Wet and Put Up Hard (10d) Located 20 feet upstream and around the corner from the *Spurt of the Movement* flake, just right of the first large chimney. Climb the narrow face with many medium-sized pockets. Avoid using the tree for aid. FA: Bob Value, 1978.

90   Spurt of the Movement (8) Start at the very obvious short, right-facing flake around the corner and 20 feet downstream from *Roads Wet.* Follow the flake and then make a series of face moves, which lead up and right to a crack system.

91   Golden Showers (10b) ★★★ Twenty feet right of *Spurt* is another attractive right-facing flake system. Climb the huecos to gain the flake. At the top of the flake move right and then back left to finish in the left-facing corner. The first ascent, even though climbed prior to the ban enforcement, was still done in classic, stealth-climbing, style—on the lead, near dusk, and during the week—to minimize the amount of time the rope was hanging over the road. FA: Bob Value/Keith Biearman, 1978.

92   Mud Bath (V2) ★★ At the short arête formed by the left edge of *Blood Bath* roof, make a series of fun moves up and right to the obvious hole. Jump from here, or continue to the top if you're on a rope. This great boulder is marred only by the oozing pigsty that sometimes forms near the base. FA: Bob Value, 1976.

Bill Crick sporting B4C4 footwear on Mudbath.
Photo by Bob Value.

93   Blood Bath (V3) Midway between *Mud Bath* and *Nitty Gritty Dirt Crack* is a nasty, hand-eating slit splitting a large, low roof. Tape up!

94   Nitty Gritty Dirt Crack (7) At the point where the main cliff turns east away from the road is an obvious short flake leading to a dirty ledge.

95   Short but Stiff (V0-V3) ★ Around the corner from *Nitty Gritty Dirt Crack*, between the road and the chimney, is a short wall with a roof 7 feet up that ends on an obvious ledge system. Approximately a dozen boulder problems exist here.

96   Dark Shadows (10a) ★ Located on the left wall of the chimney just upstream from *Jane*. Follow the arching shallow corner and face to the top. FA: Bob Value, 1976.

97   Jane (9) ★ At the left (upstream) side of the *Tarzan* roof is a line of holds leading out the left edge to the arête above. FA: Eric Guerrin, mid 1970s.

98   Tarzan (10b) ★★ Directly across the road and uphill from the Son of Foops Block is an open flat area capped by a large horizontal roof. Follow the line of flakes out the roof at its widest point. At the lip, rail left and pull over onto the face above. FA: Eric Guerrin, mid 1970s.

To find the Son of Foops block, look for the large block that overhangs the road across from the Tarzan Wall.

99   Squeal Like a Pig (V1) Located on the west side of the Son of Foops Block. Start in the right corner and traverse left across the entire back of the block. FA: Glenn Thomas, 1980.

100   Keith's Arête (V0) ★ Located on the side of the block that faces the road. Climb the blunt arête on the left edge of the face. FA: Keith Biearman, 1973.

101   Bob's Lob (V0+) Pull the short bulge and climb up the slab 5 feet right of the arête. Continue through a second bulge to the top. FA: Bob Value, 1973.

102   Road Kill (V1) ★ Climb straight up the bulges and face midway between *Bob's Lob* and *Son of Foops*. FA: Bob Value, 1973.

103   Son of Foops (V2 R) ★★★ At the widest point where the block overhangs the road, follow a line of holds out to its lip. Make a series of campus moves on decent holds to finish on top of the block. This is a high problem, and the last two intimidating moves still shut down many attempts. FA: Jack Nard, 1977.

104   Too Fooped to Poop (V0+) ★ Midway between *Son of Foops* and the right arête is a line of weakness leading up the face and over the short bulge. FA: Bill Crick, 1973.

105   Up Shit Crick (V0 R) ★★ Climb the face just left of the arête and pull through the roof at the notch. This is yet another long-standing problem that is not technically difficult but is scary because the crux comes 18 feet off the deck. FA: Bill Crick, 1978.

Sunnyside Slab

Just downstream from the Son of Foops Block (on the same side of the road) is another large boulder, the southwest face of which is a delightful, knob-covered slab. This is one of the great losses that climbers suffer due to the climbing ban on the mill side of the river.

Important Note: Climbing is prohibited in this area. These routes are listed for the historical record only.

106 Sunnyside Slab (6) ★★★ In the center of the slab is an arch. Climb the short corner up the left side of the arch. Exit onto the face above and follow a delightful line of knobs to the top.

107 Full Moon (10a) ★ Climb directly up the center of the arch and continue straight up the face above, staying right of the *Sunnyside Slab* route. FA: Bob Value, 1974.

108 Rising Sun (8) Start to the right of the arch; climb the face and eventually finish on *Full Moon.*

109 Night Fall (V0+ R) Just around the right corner from the slab is a shallow, arching corner. Poor landing. FA: Bob Value, 1974.

DOWNSTREAM

Leper/Stairs Area

This section of cliff continues downstream from Tarzan and runs to the staircase directly above the mill. It is broken in many spots; however, there are several noteworthy routes located here.

Important Note: Climbing is prohibited in this area. These routes are listed for the historical record only.

110 The Burning Zone aka The Engram (V6) ★★ To the left of *The Leper* is a pocketed, overhanging wall. In the center of the wall, make a long move from good holds to the sloping pocket and continue up slightly better holds to the ledge. If at first you get spanked, lunge, lunge, and lunge again. FA: Bob Value, 1996.

111 The Leper (V3) ★★★ Follow the cliff downstream approximately 50 feet from *Tarzan.* An obvious blunt arête is located at the point where the cliff jogs west and then back south to parallel the road. Start just left of the arête on overhanging pockets, surmount the short wall and make a long reach up and right to a position on the arête itself. Finish at the large bucket. Either jump or downclimb the crux. A classic testpiece. FA: Rick Thompson, 1980

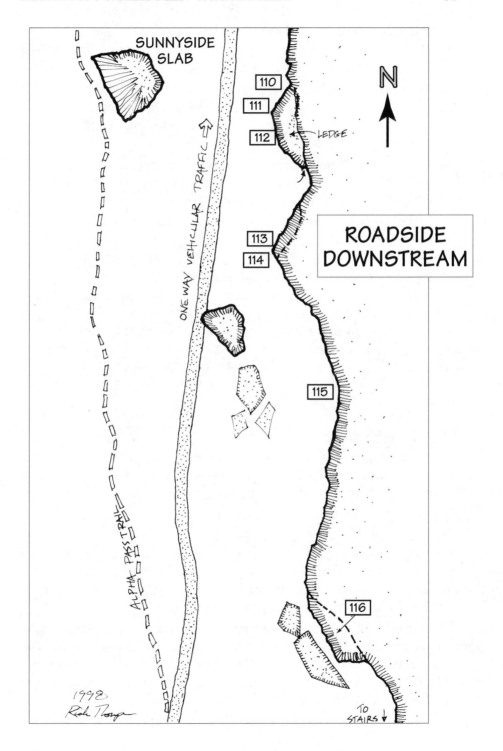

112 The One Minute Workout Wall (V0-V2) ★★ About 15 feet downstream from *The Leper* the wall turns east. This short, pocketed wall catches sun most of the day and has a number of fine pumpy boulder problems.

113 Project: Anarcheology Shares a start with *The Mummy*. About 100 feet downstream from *The Leper* is a wall characterized by a sarcophagus-shaped block at 2/3 height. Climb pockets on the left side of the wall and go straight up through bulges to finish on the arête.

114 Project: The Mummy Climb the pockets on *Anarcheology*, then move right and climb the overhang formed by the namesake block. Turn the small roof and finish up the blank face at the top.

115 Sphinxter (V2) Downstream (south) of *The Mummy* the cliff is character-ized by ledges and broken rock. Approximately 35 yards from *The Mummy* there is a short flake leading to a face. Finish at the large horizontal.

116 Coup de Grace (12a) ★ Located where the cliff turns a corner, 50 feet before the stairs. There is a large double-tiered roof perched directly above a large boulder. This route was toproped using static lines to prevent the swing into the boulder. Starting in the alcove formed under the large roof, climb the short corner and traverse right across the face to reach the lip of the first roof. Traverse left along the tier for 15 feet. At the flake line, move out to the lip of the second roof. Make a desperate move up and left to finish in the short right-facing corner. FA: Bob Value, 1983.

The Blackboard

The Blackboard is the cliff located 60 feet upstream from the "T" on Kildoo Road where you turn to descend the gorge to the mill. Dirt pullovers are located on both sides of the road after you turn, just beyond the large triangular overhang.

Important Note: Climbing is prohibited in this area. These routes are listed for the historical record only.

117 Entrance Exam (10b) ★ On the main wall just above the pullover on the right side of the road is an obvious low overhang. At the right side of this wall is a flake system. Climb the flake to the horizontal band, then continue over the short bulge to the large tree just below the top.

118 Midterm (V4 R) ★ Start 3 feet left of *Entrance Exam* at a series of three square-cut pockets. Go out the roof to the first pocket, continue past the other two and make an exciting finish up and right to the horizontal band. To descend, downclimb the start of *Entrance Exam*. The pockets on this route are often quite filthy. This is a high boulder problem. FA: Jack Nard, 1981.

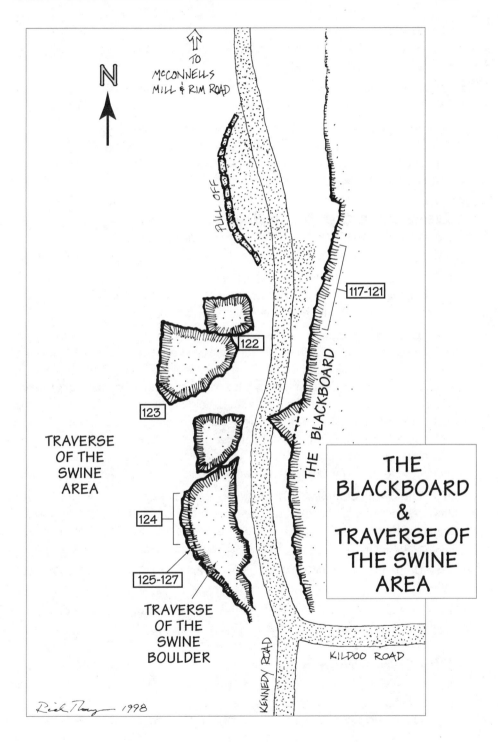

N

TO
McCONNELLS
MILL & RIM ROAD

PULL OFF

117-121

THE BLACKBOARD

122

123

TRAVERSE
OF THE
SWINE
AREA

124

125-127

TRAVERSE
OF THE
SWINE
BOULDER

THE
BLACKBOARD
&
TRAVERSE OF
THE SWINE
AREA

KENNEDY ROAD

KILDOO ROAD

Rick Thompson 1998

119   Final Exam (V4 R) ★ Several feet left of *Midterm* is a flake. Climb the flake through the roof and continue up and right on small pockets. High boulder problem. FA: Bob Value, 1982.

120   Project: Litmus Test Just left of *Final Exam* is a small pocket at the lip of the roof. Dyno for the pocket and move up and right to finish on *Final Exam*.

121   Acid Test (V2 or 11a/b) ★ On the left edge of the overhang is another obvious crack. Start to the left on pockets and make a long reach right into the crack. Follow the crack to finish at the horizontal, or continue on to the top if you are roped up. FA: Bob Value, 1981.

Traverse of the Swine Area

122   Welcome to the Swill (V0) On the left side of the road directly behind the pullover is a short overhanging wall with several moderate pocket problems.

123   Porky's Place (V0+) Located at the end of the corridor that forms the wall for *Welcome to the Swill*, at the southwest corner of the block. Start low under the roof and climb out to the arête. Follow it to the top of the block.

124   Traverse of the Swine (V4) ★★★ From *Porky's Place*, continue down-stream and west approximately 30 feet until you encounter a 60-foot long wall with a small fissure splitting it. There is a horizontal line of weakness running the entire length. Traverse this line from left to right, moving from the rounded band into pockets. After the fissure, climb small holds until it is possible to pull over the roof and finish on large sharp holds. This mighty swill route is your best bet to redline your pump meter if you only have a short time to boulder. A shorter and slightly easier traverse finishes at the fissure that splits the face. Or try moving from the right side to finish left. FA: Rick Thompson, 1982.

125   The Swine Sampler (V2) Just left of the fissure on *Traverse of the Swine* are three boulder problems. They are characterized by the only three lines of holds on the otherwise blank bulge above the traverse line. The right-hand line is about 5 feet left of the fissure. FA: Carl Samples, 1995.

126   Domestic Swine (V0+) Climb the obvious short flake. FA: Carl Samples, 1995.

127   This Little Piggy (V3/V4) ★ The left-hand problem requires a long move up to a shallow sloping dish. FA: Carl Samples, 1997.

The Ecksandstein

Located downstream of the covered bridge. The name is a pun on the Elbsandstein, East Germany's famous climbing area. Most routes in this relatively quiet area were primarily put up by Chris Eckstein and Shawn McGuirk.

Ron Kampas and Mark Van Cura on Traverse of the Swine.
Photo by Carl Samples.

To find the climbs, follow the tourist trail from the mill along the river and over the wooden footbridge. At the branch in the trail take the left fork and follow it uphill. Route 128 is the attractive, long, 10-foot high, gently overhung boulder that faces upstream on your right as you near the crest of the trail. If there is no parking available at the mill, take a left at the "T" intersection on Kildoo Road as if going to Breakneck Rocks. There is a pullover approximately 200 yards after this turn, just beyond the iron bridge. Park and then cut down over the hill to the trail. See the map for a better overview of this access.

128   Project ★★★ Sniff out a trail through sloping holds to a monodoight and more slopers, pockets and crimping. The top edge of the boulder is off limits. This 50-foot power endurance project could set a new high point in Mill bouldering standards when it is completed.

129   The Wall of Early Morning Flight (V2-V4) ★ If you continue along the trail for another 30 yards you encounter several more large boulders. The boulder on the right has an overhanging face with southern exposure that catches morning sun. There are approximately 1/2 dozen problems varying from V2 to V4 on this wall. Most involve inverted moves with long reaches off sloping suspect holds with some protruding rocks at the base. Not a good wall for the lone wolf to go scavenging for a pump—its best to bring a small pack of your fellow dingoes and a sketchpad. The west-facing side of this block offers several fun traverse eliminates up to V4 featuring one- and two-finger pocket moves.

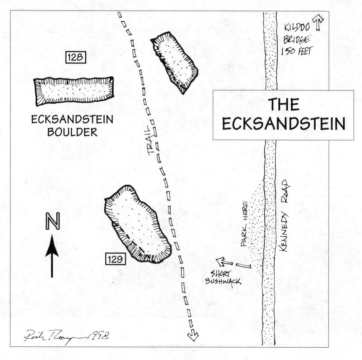

Carl Samples on a problem at The Ecksandstein.
Photo: Samples Collection.

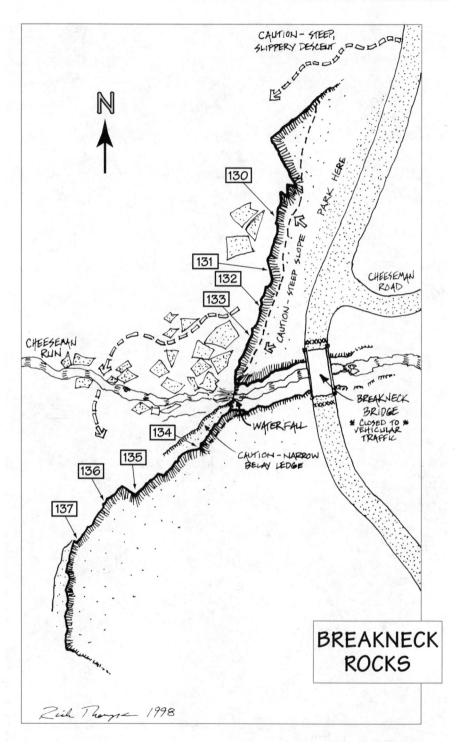

CAUTION - STEEP,
SLIPPERY DESCENT

N

PARK HERE

CHEESEMAN
ROAD

130

CAUTION - STEEP SLOPE

131

132

133

CHEESEMAN
RUN

BREAKNECK
BRIDGE
* CLOSED TO *
VEHICULAR
TRAFFIC

134

WATERFALL

135

CAUTION - NARROW
BELAY LEDGE

136

137

BREAKNECK
ROCKS

Rich Thompson 1998

CHAPTER THREE

Breakneck Rocks

Breakneck Rocks is a quiet, somewhat secluded area located about one mile downstream from the mill. To reach Breakneck Rocks follow signs to the mill. At the "T" intersection on Kildoo Road, turn left instead of following the road right down the gorge to the mill. At the next "T" intersection, turn right on Cheeseman Road, which leads to the Breakneck Bridge parking area.

Breakneck Bridge is closed to motor vehicle traffic, having died a slow death of old age and neglect. However, it does still offer a beautiful view of Breakneck Falls and serves as an access point to the cliffs located on the southern (downstream) side of the falls. Ivan Jirak, recalling the early days of climbing at Breakneck, related the following story regarding an older bridge that once graced the falls: During the 1940s, the chasm above the falls was spanned by a lovely old covered bridge. For reasons unknown, but likely having something to do with avoiding a weigh station, a driver attempted to take his 13-ton truck across the 2-ton bridge. Naturally, the truck plummeted into the ravine. The driver luckily survived; unfortunately, the old covered bridge did not.

To access the climbs on the North Wall, locate the steep descent gully on the far north (upstream) side of the cliffs. Using caution, follow it down and to the left where it passes under an impressive overhanging section of cliff. There is a project (it seems to sprout chalk from time to time) that climbs the first overhanging corner on the right edge of the overhang and then traverses out to the arête at the point of the overhang. At the point where the cliff returns to vertical there is an obvious hand crack/flake line in a corner running to the top of the cliff.

To reach the South Wall, follow the trail under the climbs on the North Wall to just before the falls. Either drop low and cross the stream at the rocky "beach" or continue to follow the upper trail. This trail continues under the falls and makes its way across some possibly dangerous, usually wet, and always awkward moves to the ledge that runs under the listed routes. Alternately, if you want to immediately reach the top of the routes to rig them, cross the bridge from the parking area. Immediately on your right will be a trail. If conditions are wet or icy, exercise extreme caution as the trail traverses dirt slopes directly above the

*Bob Value on an unnamed 5.12 at Breakneck.
Photo by Carl Samples.*

cliff. To reach the tops of the routes near the falls, stay on the low trail when it forks. To reach other routes or to get to the base of the cliffs, cut up the high trail when it forks left. Continue along the top of the ridge for approximately 75 yards until it is possible to descend the steep hillside down and right. When you first encounter the cliffs you will pass under an attractive 20-foot high boulder. A nice 5.8 ascends the blunt right hand arête. Stay high on the trail and it will deposit you on the ledge system that most routes depart from. Stay low on the trail and it will deposit you at the "beach."

To preserve some sense of adventure (the early route history here is even sketchier than the other areas) only the major routes on the main walls on both sides of the falls are listed. No first ascent data is included.

North Wall

130 Unnamed (8) ★ Climb the obvious right-angling crack and flake to the top.

130a Variation (10a) ★ Starting in the shallow corner just right of the normal start; face climb up to meet the regular route midway up the pitch.

131 Unnamed (12a) ★★ Right of Route 130 is a shallow ramp, angling up and right across the face. Follow the ramp for several moves, then climb up and left and then back right, following the clean face to the horizontal break. Make an awkward, powerful move over the break. At the next overhang, step right, then up left and over the final bulge.

132 Unnamed (11b) ★★ Starting on the ramp, follow it up and right until it is possible to climb through the notch in the overhang. Climb straight up the face on good holds. At the roof, step right and jam the obvious hand crack through the roof to the top. You can also finish through the roof via the obvious left-hand weakness. The ramp at the start may be climbed as a layback (harder) or treated as a face climb.

133 Unnamed (10b) ★★ Starting by the boulder on the right side of the wall, balance up and left to meet Route 132 at the notch in the first overhang and then continue up the face and second roof as per Route 132.

South Wall

134 Unnamed (9 - 11) ★ If following the trail from under the falls this is the first vertical wall you see after you step out from under the overhang. There are several variations on this 35-foot high wall that may require a brushing if it hasn't been climbed on recently.

135 Unnamed (4) Just right of this vertical wall is a short left-facing corner.

136 Unnamed (7) ★★★ Probably the best moderate outing at Breakneck, this climb starts under the obvious, left-facing undercling flake. Climb over some awkward bulges to the base of the short corner. Move up and left into the series of undercling moves around the flake and finish up the short ramp at the top.

137 Unnamed (10c/d) ★★ A classic route that suffers from a dirty top out. Fifteen feet right of the flake line of Route 136, at the low point in the ledge system, a series of good holds leads to a low roof. Pull the roof and follow good holds up to base of the left-facing corner. Make a series of deceptive moves up the corner and finish on a dirty exit move. With some whisking and more traffic this route would be one of the best climbs of its grade at the Mill.

Sharon Byrnes at Breakneck.
Photo by Carl Samples.

NEW ROUTE ADDENDUM

EuroChoss Wall

Unnamed (11c) ★★ On the far right side of the EuroChoss Wall is a slabby area leading over a small bulge to a short right facing corner. At the top of the corner step left and then climb over a series of bulges to the top. FA: Dean Morgan 1998.

McConnells Golden Buttress

McConnells Golden Buttress is the next prominent buttress located approximately 200 feet upstream from EuroChoss Wall. The buttress is easily identified by a line of fixed anchors following the obvious attractive overhanging arête.

Shake with No Fry (8) ★ Climb the face just left of the obvious inside corner. FA: Dean Morgan 1995

The Smell of Burning Cow Patties (7) ★ Follow the awkward sized crack up the obvious inside corner.

Fry With a Shake (10b) Climb the face just right of the corner. At the ledge make a hard move off of a mono and continue to the top. FA: Dean Morgan 1997.

McPod (11d) ★★★ Follow the line of fixed anchors up a series of overhangs on the overhanging arête to the Metolius rap station. FA: Dean Morgan 1998. This route is a fine addition to the ever-growing portfolio of steep routes in the park. If leading, the first bolt is stick clipped from the obvious ledge. If toproping please use the top anchors to avoid soil and vegetation erosion on the top of the climb. Use draws on the anchors too. Also, the lower bolts should be clipped to prevent a nasty swing into the neighboring tree.

Traverse of the Swine Area

Slick Swilly (V4 R) ★ Approximately 10 feet right of the crevasse on *The Traverse of the Swine* a series of horizontals leads up to a lone pocket on the face above. At the pocket make a long finishing move up to the horizontal band. Bad landing. FA: Carl Samples 1998.

IMPORTANT ADDRESSES AND PHONE NUMBERS

Department of Conservation and Natural Resources
McConnells Mill State Park
R.R. 2, Box 16
Portersville, PA 16051-9401
(724) 368-8091

NEAREST HOSPITAL
Butler Memorial Hospital
911 East Brady Street
Butler, PA 16001
(724) 283-6666

Directions from McConnells Mill:
Route 422 East 17 miles to Route 8 South.
Route 8 South into the town of Butler. At the 2nd traffic light make a left onto East Brady Street.
Travel approximately 1 mile and Butler Hospital is on the right.

St. Francis North Hospital
1 St. Francis Way
Cranberry Township, PA 16066
(724) 772-5300

From McConnells Mill take Route 79 South about 20 miles. Take the Cranberry exit onto Route 228 East, following signs to the Pennsylvania Turnpike. At Route 19 go left (south) to the first stoplight. Take a left. St. Francis is directly ahead.

Climbing Walls

Climb North
(412) 276-8660

Located in the North Hills, this is the closest wall to the Mill offering bouldering and toproping.

The Climbing Wall
(412) 247-7334
Located in the eastern suburbs, this facility offers lead and toprope climbing as well as bouldering.

GUIDE SERVICES AND RETAILERS
Mountain Dreams International
(412) 276-8660
Located in the South Hills, this store carrys a full line of technical, hard and soft goods and offers classes and full-service guiding to local areas like Seneca Rocks and the New River Gorge as well as more exotic locales world-wide.

The Exkursion
(412) 241-2767
Located near The Climbing Wall, this old bastion of the Pittsburgh climbing community carries a full technical line as well as offering climbing instruction.

FOOD AND LODGING
Coopers Lake Campgrounds
(724) 368-8710
Located 1 mile east of the park off Route 422

Rose Point Campgrounds
(724) 924-2415
Located 0.5 mile west of the park on Route 422.

Eppinger Restaurant
(724) 368-8383
On Route 19 1 mile from McConnells
Mill and 2 miles north of Portersville.
Features Pennsylvania Dutch
homestyle cooking. Open 24 hours.
(Watch for the big "EAT" sign.)

Kopper Kettle
(724) 368-9988
Located east of the park on Route 422.
Features classic American fare
(burgers, sandwiches).

Log Cabin Inn
(724) 452-4155
Located about 8 miles south of the
park and 2 miles before the town of
Zelienople on Route 19 South. A much
more upscale and expensive alternative to the other listed eateries, this
restaurant is usually quite busy. However you can usually get fast service if
you eat at the bar.

ROUTES BY GRADE INDEX

V4

V5

V6

ROUTES BY NAME INDEX

Features and crags are listed in captials.

ACCESS: It's every climber's concern

The Access Fund, a national, non-profit climbers organization, works to keep climbing areas open and to conserve the climbing environment. Need help with closures? land acquisition? legal or land management issues? funding for trails and other projects? starting a local climbers' group? CALL US! Climbers can help preserve access by being committed to Leave No Trace (minimum-impact) practices. Here are some simple guidelines:

• **ASPIRE TO "LEAVE NO TRACE"** especially in environmentally sensitive areas like caves. Chalk can be a significant impact on dark and porous rock—don't use it around historic rock art. Pick up litter, and leave trees and plants intact.

• **DISPOSE OF HUMAN WASTE PROPERLY** Use toilets whenever possible. If toilets are not available, dig a "cat hole" at least six inches deep and 200 feet from any water, trails, campsites, or the base of climbs. Always pack out toilet paper. On big wall routes, use a "poop tube" and carry waste up and off with you (the old "bag toss" is now illegal in many areas).

• **USE EXISTING TRAILS** Cutting switchbacks causes erosion. When walking off-trail, tread lightly, especially in the desert where cryptogamic soils (usually a dark crust) take thousands of years to form and are easily damaged. Be aware that "rim ecologies" (the clifftop) are often highly sensitive to disturbance.

• **BE DISCRETE WITH FIXED ANCHORS** *Bolts are controversial and are not a convenience* – don't place 'em unless they are really necessary. Camouflage all anchors. Remove unsightly slings from rappel stations (better to use steel chain or welded cold shuts). Bolts sometimes can be used proactively to protect fragile resources – consult with your local land manager.

• **RESPECT THE RULES** and speak up when other climbers don't. Expect restrictions in designated wilderness areas, rock art sites, caves, and to protect wildlife, especially nesting birds of prey. *Power drills are illegal in wilderness and all national parks.*

• **PARK AND CAMP IN DESIGNATED AREAS** Some climbing areas require a permit for overnight camping.

• **MAINTAIN A LOW PROFILE** Leave the boom box and day-glo clothing at home—the less climbers are heard and seen, the better.

• **RESPECT PRIVATE PROPERTY** Be courteous to land owners. Don't climb where you're not wanted.

• **JOIN THE ACCESS FUND** To become a member, make a tax-deductible donation of $25.

the ACCESS FUND

The Access Fund

Preserving America's Diverse Climbing Resources

PO Box 17010
Boulder, CO 80308
303.545.6772 • www.accessfund.org